RON & SUE RESCIGNO

WordPower Book Series

© Copyright 2021, Fig Factor Media, LLC.
All rights reserved.

All rights reserved. No portion of this book may be reproduced by mechanical, photographic or electronic process, nor may it be stored in a retrieval system, transmitted in any form or otherwise be copied for public use or private use without written permission of the copyright owner.

It is sold with the understanding that the publisher and the individual authors are not engaged in the rendering of psychological, legal, accounting or other professional advice. The content and views in each chapter are the sole expression and opinion of its author and not necessarily the views of Fig Factor Media, LLC.

For more information, contact:

Fig Factor Media, LLC | www.figfactormedia.com

Cover Design & Layout by Juan Pablo Ruiz
Printed in the United States of America

ISBN: 978-1-957058-11-5
Library of Congress Control Number: 2021923570

DEDICATION

We dedicate this book to all those who strive for CHANGE when and where it is needed. After all, what's the use of living if we don't change the world for the better after we're gone.

ACKNOWLEDGMENTS

First, we would like to thank Jackie Ruiz for including us in this wonderful exploration of words. To our son, Dominic, and daughter, Jessie, and Aunt Josie, thank you for helping us choose our word and letting us bounce ideas off of you. To all those who advised, comforted, helped, and understood the changes that have taken place in our lives since we became entrepreneurs nearly 30 years ago—Thank You!

INTRO

We're writing this book because we hope to inspire others to embrace change and move forward. Whether it's a shift in routine that allows you to have new experiences or perspectives or a change in habit that teaches you to be more adaptable, we believe change allows you to lead a more fulfilling life.

Change is inevitable.
How we respond to it determines
our future.

Change can be painful, but so can growth. And nothing is as painful as remaining stuck somewhere you don't belong. Change happens when the pain of not changing is greater than any pain that comes after.

It's not the strongest of the species that survives, nor the most intelligent, but the one most responsive to change. Don't get us wrong. To be strong and intelligent are good things, but to be able to adapt and move forward is better because life consists of constant change.

When our children left for college, we were sad. Then one day, it hit us: this is what we had been preparing them for. Growing up, leaving home, pursuing life—now that's change. And, what a beautiful, positive change it has been to see our children grow and flourish. Looking back now, we can see it was a time for all of us to learn, grow and change.

Education is really about learning and growing, which then creates change in your life and the lives of those around you. When you stop to think about it, education is how we all change, improve, and make progress together.

If you want to win at this game of life, you have to be willing to accept change and imagine the good in moving forward. Letting go of what is familiar and leaning into change can be fearful, but remaining complacent and predictable robs us of what makes life exciting.

Leaders embrace change because they believe they can always make things better.

Think about it for just a minute: is life really about change or is it about the chance to make things better? See change as an opportunity to grow, improve, and become a better, more knowledgeable person. Rather than treating change like an enemy, allow it to become your greatest ally. Open your heart to change.

When life is overwhelming, step back. Breathe. If there are changes that need to be made, you can't always see them when you are so closely involved. Picture what you want your life to be and create the steps that will get you there. No one else can make these changes in your life. You have to do the work yourself. One step at a time, slow and steady. You can change.

> "Never doubt that a small group of thoughtful, committed citizens can change the world: indeed, it's the only thing that ever has."
>
> -Margaret Mead

WE'RE REMINDED OF THIS FAVORITE QUOTE WHEN WE CONSIDER CHANGES IN OUR OWN COMMUNITY. IN OUR NEIGHBORHOOD, THE CHILDREN'S MUSEUM IN OAK LAWN WAS BUILT FROM SCRATCH BECAUSE ONE PERSON GATHERED OTHERS IN HER QUEST TO PROVIDE A FUN, INTERACTIVE SPACE. THE MUSEUM IS NOW 10,000 BEAUTIFUL SQUARE FEET WHERE CHILDREN CAN GROW AND LEARN.

ANOTHER EXAMPLE: THE COMMUNITY THAT BUILT HOPE CHILDREN'S HOSPITAL BECAUSE ONE MAN BELIEVED WE NEEDED IT AND INSPIRED OTHERS WITH THIS BELIEF. THOUGH THE MAN HAS RETIRED, TODAY THAT ONCE-SMALL HOSPITAL HAS GROWN TO BE ONE OF THE LARGEST IN THE CHICAGOLAND AREA.

If you've ever seen the movie Shrek, you probably remember how ogres are like onions because they have so many layers. In people we believe those layers are created by the way we adapt to change in our lives. Layers add maturity and experience to our lives which help us deal with change in the future.

Be the Change! Live the Change! Make the Change!

WHAT CAN BE DONE TO STRENGTHEN THE FAMILY?

WHAT CAN BE CHANGED TO END BULLYING IN SCHOOLS?

WHAT CHANGES CAN BE MADE TO HELP THE HUNGRY?

WHAT NEEDS TO CHANGE IF WE WANT TO REALLY RAISE AWARENESS ABOUT SUBSTANCE ABUSE AND MENTAL ILLNESS?

WHAT CAN YOU DO TODAY TO HELP REVERSE CLIMATE CHANGE?

WHAT CAN BE DONE TO CHANGE HOW WE APPROACH HOMELESSNESS?

THINK ABOUT IT. MAKE SOME CHANGE IN THE WORLD AROUND YOU.

ABOUT THE AUTHORS

Ron and Sue Rescigno have been happily married for over 32 years and have two wonderful children, Dominic and Jessica. In 1992, Sue Rescigno founded Rescigno's Mailing Solutions and Ron joined the business in 1994 after being in Catholic education and administration for 23 years. In 2017, they established Rescigno's Fundraising Professionals. Rescigno's specializes in helping nonprofits communicate with their donors so they can raise more money for necessary programs that make our world a better place. Ron and Sue have helped raise millions of dollars and helped foster long-term relationships with donors through multi-channel, donor-focused fundraising strategies. Ron is also the author of "The Process-Driven Annual Fund" and both have served in numerous boards and have been active members of the community always trying to make new, positive changes in the world around them.

When it comes to adapting to change, Ron and Sue have done it and are very grateful for the changes that have come to their lives. Their desire to make it through the challenges have made them closer, stronger and more adaptable to the world around them. They are grateful to God for the love of their family and friends and the opportunities He has put before them.

www.ingramcontent.com/pod-product-compliance
Lightning Source LLC
Chambersburg PA
CBHW040002290426
43673CB00078B/339